RISE ABOVE

By: Jon McNamara

Disclaimer

Table of Contents

1

Roots on the Farm

I came into this world in June 1975, the product of Beverly and Shorty McNamara's love story. The first nine years of my life unfolded on the sprawling farm in Iowa. I was surrounded by the comforting embrace of family—my parents, grandparents, and two younger sisters, Melissa and Kelli. Life on the farm wasn't just a part of my childhood; it was the essence of it.

Growing up on that farm felt like having two different lives stitched together. There were farm clothes and school clothes, each with its distinct purpose. But the farm, oh, it was more than just a place. It was where dreams and reality had their daily conversation.

Mornings kicked off with the rooster's call, a silent agreement to begin the day at the crack of dawn. Feeding the pigs and tending to the chores were rituals etched into the rhythm of our lives. But amidst the toil, there was joy in the simplicity of it all. We'd finish our tasks, and then, as kids do, we'd find our adventures, weaving hideouts and making the most of every nook and cranny.

School days were their own kind of routine, a shift from farm life to lessons and friends. My school, the one with memories I'd hold onto dearly, offered after-school stays where we'd watch movies and have our own version of chili corn – simple pleasures that made childhood magical.

Yet, amidst the everyday bustle, one soul stood as my guiding light: Grandma. Her recent passing at 97 left an irreplaceable void. She was more than a matriarch; she was my supporter, the one who helped pave my path through college. Her favorite anecdote, one she'd always recount with a twinkle in her eye, was about me, my favorite toy, and a determined walk through a rainstorm to the farm. It was moments like these that defined our bond.

Another story etched into my memory was about my grandparents and their fishing trips during summer. One fateful day, I agreed to join them despite warnings from my cousin Jimmy. Hours on a boat seemed like an eternity at that age, and it marked the last time I set sail with them. Jimmy, my confidant, and my partner in crime, was a cornerstone of my childhood. Alongside Jimmy, I navigated the farm, creating our own adventures.

Grandpa was the silent force, the nodded of approval, while Grandma, well, she was the voice of reason, albeit a repetitive one. Her playful nagging was the background music to our farm life, a melody I'd give anything to hear again. Her shouts echoed across the fields; a blend of authority and love, ensuring that we understood the delicate balance between fun and responsibility.

On my dad's side, a different world awaited—the world of welding. My paternal grandpa, a skilled welder, introduced me to the art when I was just five. His hands guided mine as I learned to weld, a skill that would become a part of my identity.

My dad, a true artisan, built our house single-handedly, epitomizing the spirit of self-reliance. Together with Grandpa, we frequented junkyards, engaging in projects that fueled my innovative spirit. It was a childhood of contrasts—farm life on my mom's side, and on my dad's, the thrill of creation and innovation.

The stories of my childhood are a tapestry woven with threads of family, freedom, and mischief. July Fourth fireworks on the Nebraska side, orchestrated by Grandpa the welder, left an indelible mark. His balloon-bursting prank, concealed in a tree, brought uproarious laughter, even from Grandma, who knew the secret.

No childhood story is ever without some misadventures. One such story was when a bottle rocket with a propeller, innocently aimed at the sidewalk, took an unexpected turn. It chased my cousin down the path, turning a routine evening into a spectacle of laughter and mild scolding. The laughter, however, lingered longer than the reprimands, a testament to the camaraderie that bound us together. Freedom was abundant, but it came with the understanding that messing up had consequences.

Grandma McNamara from my dad's side was a prankster. One of her favorite stories involved placing an ice cube behind my shirt, causing a cascade of laughter as I struggled to retrieve it. Even though it ended up in my pants, I took a bite out of it, defiantly denying any discomfort. It was these simple, lighthearted moments that defined the warmth of our family bonds.

On the farm, it was akin to a Mark Twain novel—adventures were a constant. A flat tire, a faulty bike repair, and a wild wheelie down the driveway—all part of the misadventures. The farm, a realm of freedom, ingrained in my life skills that remain invaluable.

Life back then, in the late '70s and '80s, was different. A childhood where going inside to watch TV was a rare treat, and Wonderland was an annual indulgence. The freedom granted came with the responsibility not to mess things up—an unwritten rule that shaped character.

In the tapestry of my childhood, there's a thread that weaves through the more humorous escapades on the McNamara farm—the story of a bicycle and an unintended acrobatic feat.

The farm's driveway, a lengthy stretch that cut through the heart of the fields, became the canvas for our competitions. Wheelie contests unfolded along this rural thoroughfare. The challenge was simple: who could maintain the longest wheelie down the driveway.

One day, fate intervened in the form of a flat front tire on my beloved bicycle. Determined not to let this setback hinder me from riding my bicycle, I sought the assistance of my grandpa. Together, we fixed the flat, and as a bonus, he discovered a set of brackets. Now, these seemingly mundane pieces of metal held the key to a comical episode that would echo through the years.

In my youthful ignorance, I overlooked the purpose of these brackets—to secure the wheel to the bicycle. Grandpa, equally clueless about their intended use, attached them in what he believed to be the correct manner. The result? The brackets were installed backward, a fact that would soon lead to an unintended feat of bicycle aerobatics.

With the wheel fixed, I joined my cousin for another round of wheelie contests. Little did I know that my bicycle had become a ticking time bomb of comedic chaos. As I soared down the driveway, maintaining a triumphant wheelie, the unexpected happened. The front wheel, no longer bound by the properly secured brackets, took flight.

In the spirit of true childhood bravado, I continued the wheelie, blissfully unaware that my front wheel had bounced off into the bean row beside the driveway. It was a surreal sight—me, triumphantly riding a one-wheeled bicycle down the farm driveway, while the liberated front wheel found solace among the rows of beans.

Growing up on the farm was akin to living a Mark Twain adventure, where every day held the promise of something unexpected. This incident, with its blend of hilarity and unintended acrobatics, became one of those chapters etched in the book of my childhood.

The farm, with its vast fields and unbridled freedom, taught me that life is a series of wheelies—sometimes you soar, and sometimes you find yourself in unexpected places. The lessons from those carefree days, including the importance of resilience, laughter in the face of mishaps, and the beauty of unintended adventures, remain etched in the core of my being.

As I reminisce about those formative years, I can't help but recognize the invaluable lessons learned on the farm. Independence, resilience, and the importance of family became my guiding principles. The McNamara legacy, forged in the heartland of America, laid the foundation for a journey that would eventually take me soaring through the skies.

And so, as I navigate the vastness above, I often find solace in the simplicity of a childhood spent on the farm, where roots run deep, and the wings to explore the world were first unfurled.

2

Wings of Inspiration

At six years old, I was introduced to a new world of aviation. Uncle Elden, my gateway to the skies, took me to the airport when I was just six. He was a part of the airport's support and maintenance team, ensuring runways were clean and equipment ran smoothly. During one of those visits to Sioux City, Iowa, I stumbled upon a guard base. Elden, with his rough exterior and a heart of gold, introduced me to the wonders of aviation. Little did I know that this would be the spark that would ignite my lifelong passion.

Being just a kid, I walked through helicopters and aged Hooeys, overwhelmed by the sheer magnitude of it all. Elden, unknowingly, had shown me the entry to a path I would eventually tread. The seed was planted, and from that moment, I was determined to unravel the mysteries of every aircraft, to know their ins and outs.

As time passed, my fascination with aviation grew. Elden, a tough bodybuilder with a pipe in hand, took me under his wing. In a sea of sisters, he nudged me toward a world dominated by machines and wings. His role at the airport allowed me a behind-the-scenes view, a privileged peek into the workings of the aviation world. Elden's influence kindled the flames of my ambition.

The family tradition my father set of him and me attending the Reno Air races further fueled my passion. The roar of World War II airplanes racing through the skies became a symphony that resonated with my heart. Racing motorcycles had been my previous love, but now, the call of the skies echoed louder.

Life took a turn when we moved to Winnemucca, Nevada, leaving the farmlands of Iowa behind. My dad securing a job at a coal-burning power plant marked the beginning of a new chapter. Turning ten in the vast desert of Nevada was a stark contrast to my farm-based upbringing. The challenges were immense: adapting to a new environment and a new way of life.

Moving to Nevada wasn't just a change of scenery; it was a seismic shift in my world. Dad's job at a coal-burning power plant propelled us from the agrarian landscapes of Iowa to the arid expanses of Winnemucca. My tenth birthday marked the beginning of this new chapter, and the desert welcomed me with its harsh beauty and uncharted possibilities.

As the new people in town, my mother told me not to expect a birthday party since we didn't know anyone there. But life, as we know it, doesn't always go how we plan it to. The day we moved to

Winnemucca, I became familiar with some of the kids in the neighborhood. Initially expected to pass unnoticed, my mother decided to throw me a birthday party by inviting the kids I would be attending the school with, which turned into a celebration of friendship and forging new relationships. It was the first time I ever had a birthday outside of the farmlands of Iowa and with people other than just my family. To this, it is one of my fondest memories. The bonds formed during that birthday party endured, creating a family beyond blood.

Life in Nevada wasn't a breeze. Dad toiled at the power plant, and I, the new kid in town, faced the challenge of fitting in. Picture an '80s movie scene – a jump made of cinder blocks and plywood, a group of curious kids, and me showcasing my daredevil spirit. I earned their respect that day, a symbolic leap that mirrored the leaps I'd take in my journey ahead.

But freedom came with challenges. In a town where nobody knew me, I had to carve my identity. Shyness clung to me like a second skin, but I refused to let it define me. The desert offered anonymity, a chance to shed the identity attached to my past. From a reserved fifth-grader to an Allstate football player, the transformation was both drastic and empowering. The loner became the lineman, and the shy kid found his voice on the football field and motocross tracks.

Growing up wasn't easy, and my parents, though supportive, adhered to old-school values. I was given the basics – a roof, food, and rules. Nevada became my testing ground, where I turned the unexpected into triumph. I wasn't part of the norm, but I thrived in being an outlier. The town may have initially called me the 'pig farmer' from Iowa, but I became an integral part of the community. The bonds formed in that small town, isolated from the next for 90 miles, shaped my understanding of unity and resilience. We may have started as strangers, but we couldn't escape each other's presence, and over time, we became family.

High school was a transformative period. From the farmlands of Iowa to the desert of Nevada, I hadn't ventured far. But as an Allstate football player, I tasted success. Every hurdle, every challenge, taught me a valuable lesson – the choices we make define us. Whether to press on or shy away, I chose to own my path.

As I reflect on the journey from Sioux City to Winnemucca, I realize that life is a series of decisions. Each choice shapes our destiny, and I chose to embrace the challenges, to love and be loved. Uncle Elden may not have known the extent of his impact, but his introduction to aviation set me on a course that would define my life – the life of a pilot.

3

Trials and Triumphs

Life as we know it is all about transition. Whether we like it or not, whether we know it or not, we all undergo transition at one point or another. So was the case with me. There were many phases I went through before I became the person that I am today. One such transition was the mode of vehicle I rode.

For me, the transition started with bicycles, those simple two-wheelers that whisked me away into the realm of childhood adventures. Then came motorcycles, roaring beasts that fueled my need for speed and adrenaline. But it wasn't until I discovered airplanes that my journey truly took flight.

My childhood friend, Josh, and I embarked on a venture, a nickel here, a nickel there until those coins added up to something greater. A mountain bike, the very first in Winnemucca, became the fruit of our innocent enterprise. It was a symbol of determination, a testament to the power of ambition.

The journey to aviation wasn't without its bumps. I started small, with a mini Arctic cat, a relic from the past that held the promise of freedom. But like all things, it met its end, leaving behind memories of youthful exploration. Then came the Yamaha, a gift from my parents on my tenth birthday, igniting my passion for motocross.

The road to racing wasn't smooth. A basket case race bike, a puzzle waiting to be solved, became my project, my labor of love. Each hour spent toiling away, each dollar earned, brought me closer to my dream. And when the pieces finally fell into place, I had a race bike of my own, a symbol of perseverance amidst adversity.

Motocross became my playground, my sanctuary, until one fateful day when fate dealt me a harsh blow. A crash, a brush with paralysis, left me hospitalized for three days. It was a stark reminder of the fragility of life, a lesson etched into my very being. But with the prayers of my grandmother, I defied the odds and walked out, a testament to resilience in the face of adversity.

College brought new challenges and new horizons to explore. A K 500, the most powerful dirt bike of its time, became my companion, my steed through the trials of life. And amidst it all, a friendship forged in the crucible of youth stood strong. Chris, my best friend, and my confidant, was a constant presence, a guiding light through the darkest of times.

High school, with its myriad of experiences, shaped me in ways I never thought possible. From the shy introvert to the popular Allstate football player, the journey was anything but easy. But with friends like Hornberger, Johnson, Ham, and Bill by my side, I navigated the tumultuous waters of adolescence with grace and resilience.

Bullying, a dark shadow looming over my high school years, was a hurdle I faced head-on. A punch to the jaw, a showdown that ended with a bully through a wall, left scars both physical and emotional. But it also taught me a valuable lesson – that strength lies not in aggression, but in restraint.

Anger, a tempest that brews within us all, was a force I learned to tame. Like a switch waiting to be flipped, it lay dormant, waiting for the right moment to unleash its fury. But I refused to succumb to its call, choosing instead to channel my emotions into something positive, something constructive.

Amidst the chaos of high school, I found solace in an unexpected place – the stage. Drama became my refuge, my sanctuary amidst the chaos of teenage life. From the quiet sidelines, I stepped into the spotlight, exploring the depths of emotion and expression. I joined the drama club, stepping out of my comfort zone and into a world of creativity and expression.

Participating in drama wasn't just about learning lines and hitting marks; it was about embracing vulnerability, stepping into someone else's shoes, and seeing the world through a different lens. It was a transformative experience that taught me empathy, compassion, and the power of storytelling.

Life, they say, is a journey of self-discovery, a quest to uncover the depths of our soul. As I look back on the trials and triumphs that have shaped me into the person I am today, I am grateful for every twist and turn, and every obstacle overcome. For it is in the face of adversity that we discover our true strength, our true purpose. And though the road ahead may be long and fraught with challenges, I face it with courage and conviction, knowing that with each step, I grow stronger, wiser, and more resilient than before.

4

Defying Expectations

Life has a curious way of challenging our dreams, often testing our resolve in ways we never imagined. For me, the journey to the skies began with a simple declaration to my high school counselor – I wanted to be a pilot. But instead of encouragement, I was met with skepticism, even derision. "You'll never be a pilot," he said, dismissing my aspirations with a wave of his hand.

I remember that day vividly, sitting across from my counselor as he flipped through my applications, his expression one of disdain. "Your grades are too good," he scoffed. "You need to go be an engineer. You'll never be a pilot." Little did I know, those words would ignite a fire within me, propelling me forward against all odds.

I refused to be deterred. Armed with determination and a thirst for adventure, I embarked on a journey to prove the doubters wrong. As an Allstate football player and an honor roll student, I had already conquered every challenge thrown my way. Yet, despite my achievements, the path to my dream seemed clouded with uncertainty.

The awards night was a bitter pill to swallow. As each scholarship was handed out, I felt the weight of expectation bearing down on me.

Despite excelling in academics and sports, I found myself overlooked when it came to scholarships and opportunities. While my friends celebrated their full rides to prestigious colleges, I sat alone in the empty auditorium. When the night came to an end, I was left with nothing but tears and a sense of betrayal. All my hard work and dedication seemed to count for nothing. Ms. Kennedy, the drama teacher, bestowed upon me an unexpected honor – the award for "most improved."

It was a moment of reckoning, a turning point in my journey. As I sat in the empty auditorium, tears streaming down my face, I realized that no one was going to hand me my dreams on a silver platter. If I wanted to fly, I had to find a way to make it happen on my own.

As I returned to school on Monday, I was surprised to find several teachers inquiring about my lack of scholarship applications. "Hey man, we were waiting for you to submit your application," they said, confusion evident in their voices. It was then that I realized the extent of my counselor's betrayal – he had discarded my applications without my knowledge, robbing me of opportunities I had worked so hard to attain.

Faced with the harsh reality of my counselor's betrayal, I realized I had to forge my own path. But before fully committing to my dream of becoming a pilot, I decided to pursue engineering at Peninsula College. My parents had saved up money for my education, and I felt obligated to follow the path that had been laid out for me. But fate had other plans, and a near-fatal motorcycle accident forced me to confront the harsh reality that engineering was not my calling.

It was then that I made a decision – to forge my own path, to chart a course that was uniquely mine. I took odd jobs, saving every penny I could in pursuit of my dream. A chance encounter led me to a job on a crab boat in the Bering Sea, where I would spend grueling months battling the elements and testing the limits of my endurance. It was a harsh and unforgiving environment, but amidst the chaos, I discovered a strength within myself I never knew existed.

The days spent on the crab boat were some of the toughest I've ever endured. Long hours, seasickness, and the constant danger looming over us tested my limits, pushing me to the brink of exhaustion. But amidst the chaos, I discovered a strength within myself I never knew existed.

When I returned home empty-handed after quitting work on the crab boat, I had no idea what life had in store for me. There was uncertainty surrounding me, and I didn't know which direction to turn—amidst it all, moments of pure joy and camaraderie kept me grounded. Like the unforgettable house parties with my best buddy Jared, where we'd gather on the roof, surrounded by friends and laughter, watching the sunrise as we dared to dream of a future filled with endless possibilities.

During one of the house parties, watching the sunrise on the roof with Jared, I decided to follow my passion for flying and to become a pilot. We made a pact – he would start his own drilling company, and I would pursue my dream of becoming a pilot. It was a leap of faith, a commitment to charting our own destinies in the face of uncertainty.

Having no money to enroll in an aviation program, I moved back home to Winnemucca to live with my parents. When I told them about the decision to become a pilot, they simply replied, "If anyone can do it, it's you." It was all I needed to hear to keep going and work for it even harder than before.

After my parents' unwavering support, my resolve to become a pilot became firmer. It was a choice that filled me with both excitement and trepidation, but I knew deep down that it was the path I was meant to follow. When I shared my decision with my grandmother, expecting skepticism or resistance, I was met with unwavering support and pride. Her belief in me bolstered my confidence and reaffirmed my resolve to pursue my dreams against all odds. She even went the extra mile to buy all my books, a gesture that touched my heart and fueled my determination to succeed.

Knowing there was no other way than saving up myself to go to an aviation school, I set out to forge my own path. I found employment at a gold mine, where I worked tirelessly to support myself and save for the future. I started from the very bottom, working as a ditch miner and rising to the rank of heavy equipment engineer. It was a humbling experience, but it taught me the value of hard work and perseverance in the face of adversity. However, when the mine faced cutbacks due to plummeting gold prices, I found myself among those laid off.

Yet, from the ashes of adversity rose a new opportunity. With the severance pay I received, I made the bold decision to pursue my lifelong dream of becoming a pilot. I packed my bags and headed to Oklahoma, where I enrolled in Spartan College of Aeronautics and Technology.

The days spent at flight school were some of my life's most challenging yet exhilarating. From navigating the intricacies of flight mechanics to mastering the art of aerial maneuvers, every moment brought me closer to my goal. And when I finally earned my private pilot's license, it was a moment of triumph unlike any other.

But my journey was far from over. With each new milestone, I encountered fresh challenges and obstacles along the way. Yet, through sheer determination and unwavering resolve, I pushed forward, fueled by the dream of soaring among the clouds one day.

Today, as I reflect on the trials and triumphs that have brought me to where I am, I am filled with gratitude for every twist and turn, every obstacle overcome, for it is in the journey itself that we discover our true strength and resilience, our ability to defy expectations and chart our own course through life's turbulent waters. I am proud to be the first person in my family to hold a bachelor's degree, breaking free from the norms and paving the way for future generations to pursue their dreams without limitations. And though my grandmother may no longer be with us, her unwavering belief in me continues to inspire me to reach for the stars and never give up on my dreams.

5

Wings of Freedom

The air in Port Angeles, Washington, held promises of adventure and liberation. As I stood on the rugged coastline, looking out at the vast expanse of the Pacific Northwest, I knew deep within my soul that my destiny awaited me beyond the horizon.

Fresh from my days on the crab boat, I found myself yearning for something more. The repetitive routine of hauling traps and battling the elements left me feeling restless, aching for a taste of the boundless freedom that only the sky could offer.

It was on January 2nd, 1996, that I took my first steps towards that freedom. The day was etched into my memory like a beacon of hope, and a symbol of newfound possibility. As I climbed into the cockpit of an airplane for the very first time, I felt a surge of excitement and nerves coursing through my veins.

With every haul of the traps and every gut-wrenching storm, the dream of flight grew stronger within me. It was a whisper in the wind, and a beacon of light in the darkness that was urging me to reach for something more that was beyond the confines of the boat.

And so, with determination burning bright within my soul, I scraped together every penny I had saved and made my way to the airport. The scent of jet fuel filled the air, mingling with the profound sense of excitement and anticipation that pulsed through my veins.

Approaching the flight instructor, I could feel my heart pounding in my chest. This was it – the moment when I would take control of my destiny and soar into the unknown.

The instructor greeted me with a warm smile. Perhaps he had sensed the mix of nerves and excitement that danced in my eyes. With steady hands, I handed over the money for my first flight lesson.

As I climbed into the cockpit of the waiting airplane, a rush of adrenaline surged through my veins. The controls felt foreign beneath my fingertips, yet there was also a sense of familiarity, as if I had been born to fly.

With the instructor's guidance, I taxied onto the runway. My heart was pounding in my chest as the anticipation built to a fever pitch. This was the moment I had been waiting for – the moment when I would leave behind the confines of the earth and take to the skies.

As the engine roared to life and the wheels left the ground, a surge of emotion washed over me. The ground fell away beneath me, a blur of colors and shapes as I soared into the vast expanse of the sky. "Alright, let's do this," I said to myself, trying to steady my nerves as the instructor's calm voice filled the cockpit.

"Just remember what we went over in class," he reassured me. "You've got this."

With a deep breath, I pushed the throttle forward, feeling the aircraft surge forward with a burst of speed. I felt the loss of friction as the wheels left the ground, and suddenly, I was airborne, soaring into the vast sky.

For the first time in my life, I felt truly alive. The wind whipped through my hair, and the sun kissed my skin. With each passing moment, I felt myself becoming one with the airplane. It felt like a part of something greater than myself.

As I flew higher and higher, the worries and stresses of everyday life fell away, replaced by a sense of clarity and purpose. This was where I belonged, where I was meant to be – in the cockpit of an airplane, chasing dreams and embracing the unknown with open arms.

However, amidst the exhilaration of flight, there was also a profound sense of gratitude. Gratitude for the journey that had brought me to this moment, for the struggles and sacrifices that had shaped me into the person I am today.

As the sun dipped below the horizon and the stars emerged in the darkening sky, I made a silent vow to myself. I would become a pilot, not just for the thrill of it, but because it was my destiny. And so, with each subsequent flight, I soared higher and higher, chased dreams farther and farther, and embraced my destiny with open arms.

Now, nearly three decades and eleven thousand hours of flight time later, I look back on that fateful day with gratitude and awe. It was the day I found my wings... the day I embraced my destiny..., and the day I became a pilot.

And though the journey was long and challenging, I wouldn't change a single moment of it, for it was in the skies that I truly found myself.

At that moment, I realized that flying wasn't just about reaching a destination. It was about embracing the journey, embracing the unknown, and embracing the person I was meant to be. And as I soared through the endless expanse of the sky, I knew that I had finally found my calling, my passion, my purpose.

6

First Flight

The journey of a lifetime often begins with a single flight... with a leap of faith into the unknown. And for me, that leap came after I traded in my football cleats for the cockpit of an airplane.

The memories of my first flight lesson lingered in my mind, which were a constant reminder of the thrill and wonder that awaited me in the skies above. With newfound determination coursing through my veins, I embarked on a quest to explore the world from a whole new perspective.

My destination was the vibrant city of Las Vegas, where dreams were born, and fortunes were won and lost in the blink of an eye. From the bustling streets of Reno, I soared through the clouds toward the neon-lit skyline of Sin City.

As the airplane banked and dipped through the air, I couldn't help but marvel at the sights unfolding beneath me. The glittering lights of the Las Vegas Strip stretched out before me like a river of stars, casting their magic spell over all who dared to dream.

Touching down in Vegas felt like stepping into another world, where anything was possible and reality blurred with fantasy. From the vibrant casinos to the world-class entertainment, every corner of the city pulsed with energy and excitement.

But amidst the glitz and glamour, there was also a sense of humility, which was a reminder of the journey that had brought me here. From the humble beginnings on the crab boat to the exhilaration of flight, every step had shaped me into the person I was meant to be.

As I wandered the streets of Vegas, marveling at the sights and sounds that surrounded me, I couldn't help but feel a sense of gratitude wash over me. I am grateful for the opportunity to explore, to discover, and to chase my dreams wherever they may lead.

As I gazed up at the twinkling lights of the city, I knew that this was just the beginning of a journey that would take me to places beyond my wildest imagination. For in the boundless expanse of the sky, there are no limits, no boundaries, only endless possibilities waiting to be discovered.

Learning to fly is like embarking on a journey of discovery. Each lesson was a stepping stone towards mastering the skies. For me, that journey began in a small, confined area, where the roar of the engine and the whisper of the wind were my only companions.

The airplane I visited for the very first time was a humble trainer. Its wings were stretched out like a welcoming embrace as I approached. It may not have been the biggest or the fastest plane in the sky, but to me, it represented freedom, possibility, and the fulfillment of a lifelong dream.

As I climbed into the cockpit, the familiar scent of aviation fuel filled my nostrils, mingling with the excitement and anticipation that bubbled within me. This was it. That was the moment I had been waiting for… the moment when I would take control of my destiny and soar into the unknown.

But as the engine roared to life and the airplane taxied down the runway, a sense of nervous excitement fluttered in the pit of my stomach. It was a feeling akin to the first time you take the wheel of a car, a mixture of exhilaration and trepidation as you navigate uncharted territory.

The instructor's voice crackled over the intercom, guiding me through the intricacies of the air maneuvers we would be practicing. From stalls to steep turns, each maneuver was like a puzzle waiting to be solved, a challenge to be overcome with skill and precision.

And so, with hands steady on the controls and eyes focused on the horizon, I took to the skies. The airplane responded to my touch with grace and agility, soaring through the air like a bird in flight. It was a feeling unlike any other. A sense of freedom and exhilaration lifted my spirits and set my soul on fire.

But amidst the thrill of flight, there was also a sense of responsibility, which was a reminder that every action had consequences, and every decision could mean the difference between life and death. It was a humbling realization, but one that only fueled my determination to become the best pilot I could be.

As the lesson drew to a close and the airplane touch had down gently on the runway, I couldn't help but feel a sense of pride swell within me. Despite the nerves and the uncertainty, I had faced my fears and emerged stronger on the other side.

And as I climbed out of the cockpit, my heart was still racing with the adrenaline of flight. I knew that this was just the beginning of a journey that would take me to the highest heights and the farthest reaches of the sky. For in the boundless expanse of the heavens, there are no limits or boundaries, but only endless possibilities waiting to be discovered.

7

Career Ordeal

Becoming a pilot wasn't just a career change for me; it was a transformation of my entire life. From the humble beginnings of living in a house and working on crab boats, I had dared to dream of something greater. And now, as I sit in the cockpit of a 747, flying across the world, I realize just how far I've come.

The decision to pursue my passion for flying wasn't easy. It required sacrifice, determination, and a willingness to step out of my comfort zone. But with each milestone I reached, and with each hurdle I overcame, my life began to change in ways I never thought possible.

Gone were the long days spent toiling on the crab boat, the endless monotony broken only by the occasional glimpse of the horizon. In their place were the boundless skies, where every flight brought a new adventure, a new challenge, and a new sense of freedom.

Flying a 747 was a dream come true. The sheer size and power of the aircraft filled me with awe and reverence, reminding me of the incredible journey that had brought me here. From the cramped confines of a fishing boat to the spacious cockpit of a jumbo jet, my life had been transformed in ways I could never have imagined.

But it wasn't just about the airplanes or the destinations; it was about the people I met along the way, and the friendships forged in the crucible of the skies. Whether it was sharing stories with fellow pilots during layovers or marveling at the wonders of the world with passengers, every interaction left an indelible mark on my soul.

And then, there was my family, who had stood by me through every twist and turn of this incredible journey. Their love and support had been the wind beneath my wings, propelling me ever higher towards my dreams. And now, as I fly across the world, I carry them with me in my heart, which is a constant reminder of the blessings that surround me.

I wish I could put into words the profound impact that becoming a pilot has had on my life. It's more than just a job... it's a calling... a passion... a way of life. It's about chasing dreams, defying expectations, and embracing the unknown with open arms.

So, as I sit here in the cockpit, cruising at thirty-thousand feet above the earth, I can't help but feel a sense of gratitude wash over me. I am grateful for the opportunities I've been given, the people I've met, and the experiences that have shaped me into the person I am today.

And as I look out at the vast expanse of the sky, stretching out before me like an endless canvas, I know that the journey is far from over. There are still adventures to be had, dreams to be chased, and horizons to be explored. And I wouldn't have it any other way.

Becoming a pilot was more than just choosing a career path for me. It was a testament to resilience, determination, and the unwavering pursuit of a dream. As I look back to the journey that brought me to where I am today, I can't help but marvel at the twists and turns life has thrown my way.

Graduating right after the attacks of September 11th was a stark reminder of the fragility of life and the unpredictability of the future. Despite earning my bachelor's degree and obtaining all my ratings, the aviation industry came to a grinding halt in the wake of the terrorist attacks. Overnight, my dreams of soaring through the skies were dashed, leaving me adrift in a sea of uncertainty.

With no flying jobs in sight, I found myself at a crossroads, where I was forced to confront the harsh reality of starting over. Returning to Winnemucca, Nevada, and moving back in with my parents felt like a step backward. It was a bitter pill to swallow after years of hard work and dedication.

But adversity has a way of revealing our true strength, and I refused to let the setbacks define me. Instead, I rolled up my sleeves and set to work, building a new life from the ground up. From working in construction to laboring in gold mines, every job was a stepping stone towards my ultimate goal.

I'll never forget the moment when I started as a humble trash dumper and rose through the ranks to become a heavy equipment mechanic. It was a test of my perseverance and resilience. It was a reminder that no matter how dire the circumstances may seem, there is always a way forward.

When the price of gold plummeted, and I found myself facing yet another setback, I refused to be defeated. Instead, I seized the opportunity to pursue higher education, and enrolled myself in college at the age of twenty-three to pursue my bachelor's degree.

The road to graduation was fraught with challenges and obstacles, but with each hurdle I cleared, I grew stronger, more determined, and more resilient. And when I finally walked across that stage to receive my degree, it was a moment of success unlike any other.

But even as I celebrated my academic achievements, the shadow of 9/11 loomed large, and it cast doubt on my future once again. With flying jobs still scarce, I had no choice but to bide my time, waiting for the winds of change to shift in my favor.

And yet, through it all, I remained steadfast in my belief that someday, somehow, I would take to the skies once again. I had learned the hard way that the journey of becoming a pilot wasn't just about flying planes, but it was about embracing the challenges, overcoming the obstacles, and proving to myself and the world that nothing could ground my spirit of adventure.

So here I am, years later, soaring through the clouds with a renewed sense of purpose and gratitude.

The road may have been long and arduous, but every twist and turn has led me to this moment, where I realize that resilience and determination are the true keys to unlocking the sky.

And as I look back on the journey that brought me here, I can't help but smile, knowing that the best is yet to come.

8

MY FLIGHT PATHS AND MY FORTUNE

The airstrip at Winnemucca was eerily quiet, as though a fold of bliss had enveloped it into silence. Here I was, right out of college with a degree and an ambition soaring high; how was I to know that I'd meet an unexpected reality that would close some doors while opening many others?

The aviation industry had torn and tattered post-9/11, and so was my dream of flying those commercial planes. Out of college was a good experience; I had a degree and high spirits, but being out of a job was devastating.

With nothing to do, I was in my hometown, teaching others how to fly a plane, which was not what I had aimed for.

A freelance flight instructor was never something I had wanted to be; but with the limited options that I had, what else could I do?

Nothing glamorous, nothing fancy, but that was what I had to do. It was where I had ended up. My days were spent at the local airport, crouched down in a small, somewhat worn-out office, waiting for students to arrive so I could begin my lessons.

The nature of my job was basic and very straightforward: teaching people the basics of flying, the mechanics of the aircraft, and the absolute thrill of being in control of a plane. As a teacher, I was still flying planes, which was better than having nothing to do.

Through each lesson, I tried to bring the same passion I had felt when I first took to the skies. I had felt the adrenaline pumping my blood stream and my heart running like a wild horse.

I have heard people say, "nothing lasts forever," and that goes for my circumstances as well. It was one fine autumn afternoon when an opportunity knocked on my door.

Dr. Michael Lewis, a renowned physician with a flair for the eccentric, arrived at the airstrip. He was quite a character—he had more unconventional hobbies than a medical practice, and his latest venture was a tamale festival in Elko. He was known for his grand adventures, and he had brought his own plane for the trip, which was rather thrilling.

"My friend, my friend," he had clapped my back with a wide grin and added, "I need your help, really. I am actually heading towards Elko for a festival, and you are coming with me."

"You have made all the preparations?" I asked. My question had a hint of curiosity, to which he nodded in agreement.

"I have, and we are all set to leave," he answered with a wide grin.

"I understand. I am just thinking it's a bit too…"

"Too quick? Bit too quick? Life is full of surprises, isn't it? So, what do you say?"

"I agree," I shook my head.

"So? Yes, or no?" He asked me again.

How could I refuse?

Elko was about an hour's flight away; the aircraft that Dr. Lewis had with him was a big deal. It was a large, multi-engine plane—much that was far bigger than anything I had ever flown before in my life. I wanted to refuse, but the thrill of the challenge was too tempting to turn down.

The next morning, when the doctor was all sober and ready, I was in the cockpit of the beautiful machine. The engine sound breathed life into my passion; it was exhilarating and exciting.

"You got this, you really do!" Dr. Lewis said to me.

"Thanks," I appreciated his comment.

We were ready to take off, and take off we did. The aircraft soared into the clear sky, piercing through the clouds. I felt larger than life, almost like an out-of-body experience. Glancing from my window, I marveled at the view below; it was such a breathtaking experience that it instantly changed my mood.

Nevada stretched out in a vast expanse of browns and greens with warm rays of sun gently touching every object in sight.

I figured at that very moment that flying such a large plane was a different experience entirely — much different than what I had flown most of my life. With a heavy engine like that, every control seemed to demand more power, and every maneuver required a careful touch of the pilot.

I knew I had to be subtle and discreet with my position in the place; one wrong move and it would have gone down the drain.

Time went by. Dr. Lewis and I briefly chatted before the take-off. Finally, when we approached Elko, I noticed that the landscape had entirely transformed. Things looked so different from what I had seen when I was taking off.

We touched down on a runway that shook us slightly, which was an indication that we had reached our destination safely. One of the riskiest times in a pilot's career was also one of the most thrilling times for me: the landing and the take-off. I felt alive with excitement.

"I am off. See you." Dr. Lewis jumped out, eager to dive into the festivities, leaving me alone in the cockpit to keep the plane ready for the trip back home.

I took care of all that needed to be taken care of while Dr. Lewis was busy sampling tamales and mingling with those in the festival. For what seemed like some minutes, I stayed in the cockpit and observed all that was happening below. It was a rare moment of peace and quiet, a moment of me-time, as I put it. I briefly reflected on how far I was from home.

Taking a deep breath, I left the plane and joined Dr. Lewis and the others. The festival was pretty exciting – I loved it.

Once we were done with it, it was time for us to return home; that was a blend of relief and satisfaction.

I was able to pilot the large aircraft back to Winnemucca with lots of memories. Dr. Lewis was tired but very content with how smoothly things had gone.

"Are we landing?" He had asked me.

"Yes," I said as I pulled the gear. We touched down as smoothly as we had taken off, and I felt a surge of pride in what I had accomplished.

"You did it," Dr. Lewis smiled at me and patted my shoulder.

"Thanks again."

"I trust you to do the right thing." He added as he left the plane.

What I hadn't told him was that the flight to Elko and back home was more than just another job for me; it was a demonstration of how skilled I was and how I could handle a different plane.

It was really bold and daring to agree to such a daunting task, but it was totally worth it. Words of Dr. Lewis rang in my ears: *you really did it.* I had managed to navigate a large aircraft, one with which I was not accustomed to, with perfect ease and confidence. I had also proven my talent, my passion, and my capabilities. Above all, I had the chance to view the perfect sunset when I was taking off. It had deepened my love for flying.

I was ready for whatever challenge came next.

9

My Adventures with The Burning Man

I'd always have a daring spirit, one that was bold and strong. I was never one to turn away from an obstacle or a tough challenge, so when the opportunity was there for me to dive headfirst into the world of Burning Man, I just knew that I had to seize it. There was no way I would have let that pass.

It was the year 2004, the festival of Burning Man was getting more popular day by day. Basically, it is a festival that lasts around a week and takes place in the desert. There are performances and camps, and the attendees, called "Burners," gather to create a temporary city where art, creativity, and self-expression are celebrated.

As I said, the year 2004 witnessed the festival with enthusiasm and appreciation by the attendees, but there was a gap in the market, and that was transportation. This was my chance to be myself and make a mark, and I was determined to make it count.

I can still remember the first time when I thought about offering charter services at the festival of Burning Man. It was more than just a crazy idea; it was a well-assessed and calculated risk.

The festival, with its extensive and beautiful desert landscape, seemed like the perfect place to do something exceptional. I wasn't just going to be another pilot flying in and out of the Black Rock Desert like everyone was. I wanted to create something memorable and something that was unthinkable.

The plan was really simple yet a bit too ambitious: set up a charter service focusing on convenience and comfort. So, I arranged for a duplex setup, which was essentially about creating a temporary airport in the middle of the desert.

Now, that was something!

I knew I was doing something extraordinary.

It was a very challenging idea, but somehow, I managed to get it all together. It was $99 for a seat, and festival lovers and goers could enjoy a ride that was as much a part of the Burning Man experience as the festival itself.

I was very excited about that idea, not realizing that the process of setting it all up would be demanding and exhausting. I had to work almost round the clock, coordinating with multiple teams while making sure that everything was going just the way I had planned.

Since I had set out to do something different, I wanted to be exceptionally different; I didn't just want to be another service; I wanted to be part of the festival's core and spirit.

I had high hopes, but the real question was whether the community would welcome my crazy idea and appreciate all the efforts I put into it.

As I had expected, not everyone was thrilled about my idea. The festival was always for how it took us away from all the commercialization, and my plan of charter service was not welcomed by everyone. It was considered an intrusion into their traditions and culture.

There were murmurs of dissatisfaction and discontent, and I was warned beforehand that I might have to face some level of hostility. The community was notorious for its confrontation with what they considered capitalism's violation of their utopian area.

Despite the initial reaction, my project started to gain a grip. The infrastructure that I'd set up turned out to be a great asset for a lot of attendees. The service that I offered was smooth and efficient, and it was appreciated by a large segment of the crowd, much to my surprise. I was at the center of a growing buzz. The critics were there, but they were not as popular as was my idea. Their voice was being drowned out by the voices of those who found real value in what I was offering to them.

I could see marks of relief on their faces when they realized they didn't have to pass through the desert's coarse topography on their own.

One of the most memorable moments was when I saw a group of festival-goers stepping out from the aircraft. They were thrilled, high-fiving each other and laughing. It was a moment of victory for me.

That scene perfectly summarized the spirit of Burning Man — a mixture of chaos, creativity, art, and celebration. I realized then that despite the criticism and challenges, I had done something special. Much more special than any other pilot could do.

I stayed with the Burning Man operation for several years, improving and enhancing the features of the service. The initial skepticism gradually faded as more and more people began to like what I had to offer them. I felt like a pioneer, creating a new path in a place where orthodox traditions were valued over everything.

In the end, the journey was more than just a business project; it was an assessment of how modernization could coexist with old traditions. It was worth every ounce of effort I had put in.

In retrospect, I understand that the experience was not just about the charter service or the logistical challenges. It was about pushing my boundaries and finding new ways to mix into a community that was really protective of its identity. I had become part of the Burning Man legacy, and that was something I'd always be proud of.

10

REBIRTH FROM THE ASHES: NEW BEGINNINGS

I remember there was a time when I had done nothing for a few days; I just sat in my chair and took deep breaths. It was a moment of reflection, sort of. I've never been one to talk much about personal matters, but today felt different. The questions were straightforward, yet they were attached to memories I hadn't revisited in years.

I never had any conflicts with my business partner, I thought to myself. My partner is still my best friend. So why did I quit? I wondered if quitters are always losers? Or people who leave one thing for another, are they at the losing end?

My mental faculties told me to shut up, and not give it a second thought, but with not much to do that day, I was forced to recall past events.

It wasn't about any professional issue or any tension—it was just time. I told myself. And I was right.

I've never really had any tension with anyone in my career. It wasn't a situation where something was taken from me, or I took something from someone else. It was more like an apple falling from a tree. When it's ripe, it falls—it's just the natural order of things. It was my time to fall.

When I say fall, I don't mean defeat, or surrender. In fact, it is quite the opposite. Somehow, my life had never been a competition, it was more of a journey from one destination to another. Falling from the tree was a part of it – I never got to the bottom because I was a failure, instead, it was my rebirth.

I've never quit a job. Jobs have disappeared, but I've never just walked away from them. That's not me, that's not how I did things in my life. Life has a rhythm you know? It's like there's always something there to catch me when I take a step. Maybe it's luck, or maybe it's something else. But every time, there's been a path beneath my feet.

I am very proud of the things I got to do in my life, which are full of thrills, adventure, and nail-biting twists and turns, and when I say I am proud, I do not mean in arrogance, I meant it as a way to know my worth.

I remember I had felt a wave of relief and comfort sweep through me, which was odd, since I was not depressed or worried about anything to begin with.

I thought back to the twists and turns my career had taken. "or 20 years, jobs just came to me. Can I pertain that to a stroke of luck? It could be. Or maybe my talent and potential. I knew I was born different. I had wings and I believed I could fly.

For my professional life, I never had to apply for a position, with my luck and my hard work. This job, flying the 747, was the first one I actually had to interview for. Before that, it was always, 'Come join us, or come work for us.' And that was it.

I've been fortunate, no doubt. But I also worked my ass off to build my reputation. So it was partly the stars aligning to give me good luck, and primarily, my own hard work and talent behind it all.

As I was sitting there, my thoughts drifted to a story that had become one of the defining moments of my life—a day that tested my determination and pushed me to the edge.

I was flying a 402 out of Elko, Nevada—a twin-engine, unpressurized plane. One day, the right engine started acting up, and it wasn't just a hiccup. It was a full-on failure. There I was, no co-pilot, just me and a dead engine. You go through the checklist, try everything, but it was clear—the engine was gone.

My heart beat had picked pace as I relived the traumatic experience. In that moment, I didn't know if it was bad fuel or something else. I didn't know if the other engine was going to fail too. There was an airport nearby, and I made the decision to land. But let me tell you—when you know you're about to die, it's like you slip into another timeline, like you're not supposed to be here anymore.

As I said before, it was always rebirth. The apply falling to the ground was a symbol of a new seed, a new tree of new beginnings sprouting from the ground.

Rebirth.

I shook my head - the memory was still vivid. That was on a Monday. By Wednesday, they had called me, saying the plane was fixed and ready to go. I told them, 'No way.' But they kept pushing. The chief pilot, the director of maintenance, everyone was on me to take the plane up again.

Eventually, I gave in. I took off, got maybe 100 feet off the ground, and the engine sputtered again. It was like the universe was testing me. There was an RV park ahead, power lines to the left, and town to the right. I knew I was going to crash. But just as I was about to pull back the throttle, something incredible happened—a dust devil picked me up and gave me just enough lift to clear the power lines.

That 40 feet saved my life.

I let the gravity of the moment settle in. I don't even remember landing. But my fortunate stars had aligned perfectly, or so they say with the zodiac and all. Not much of a believer, but the thrilling moment of having that near-death experience was enthralling for me. When I landed, the fire trucks were already there. It was all so surreal.

That day in Elko, I realized just how close I came to losing everything. It's funny, in a way—how life works out.

The room was silent as my story hung in the air. I've never been one to seek the spotlight, but there was a quiet pride in my inner voice.

I had made it! Many times, over and over.

And with that, the chapter of my life that almost ended in the Nevada desert is now captured in words—preserved, not forgotten.

11

The Unforeseen Path

After the Burning Man episode, everything changed in ways I that hadn't anticipated. I was one of the first people to get involved in setting up the infrastructure there. It was a crazy idea and wild—trying to bring some order and structure to a place that thrives on chaos and mess. I partnered up with this guy who, in hindsight, wasn't the best choice.

From day one, he seemed to have a chip on his shoulder about the whole thing, constantly calling me a "capitalist pig" and saying people would end up throwing eggs at me, which was disappointing for me. But I had given my word. I promised to see the project through for at least a year, and I intended to keep that promise.

As my year was wrapping up, I took some time to be with my family. I believed it was time to unwind with those closest to me.

My parents lived a couple of hours away, and my son was just a baby — one or two years old. Those moments were precious, holding him and feeling the weight of my responsibilities, both as a father and as someone who always ends up on some kind of wild adventure. I could feel his tiny palms and curious eyes gripping me. I thought I might finally have a little bit of peace and quiet.

Then, out of the blue, I got a call. It was a man I didn't know, and he kept calling me "Johnny Mac" like we were old friends, or at least, very deep acquaintances.

"We need you to fly out immediately," he said.

I remember sitting there, staring at the phone, thinking who the hell is this guy, and why is he calling me during Thanksgiving weekend? I told him straight up that I couldn't just drop everything and leave; I had to wait until January. I needed time to think.

The funny thing is, I've never applied for a job in my life — not until the one I hold now. My career has always had a way of unfolding without me having to chase anything down.

After Burning Man, for example, I was quickly pulled into another project, another company. They wanted me to help them platform, to build something from scratch, just like I'd done before.

I was on their radar, and they wanted me right then. But I had a family, commitments that went beyond work. I couldn't just up and leave whenever someone called. That didn't sit right with me.

The next job I took was unlike anything I'd experienced before. I used to call it my "death devil" job because, truthfully, I came close to dying more times than I care to count.

It was as if every day was another brush with fate, another moment where I thought, "This is it. This is where it all ends." But somehow, by some miracle or sheer stubbornness, I made it through. I always had this feeling in my gut that my number was up, but I kept surviving, kept moving forward.

People sometimes ask why I left that company, or how long I was unemployed. The truth is, I was never really without work. I had built that company from the ground up, put my blood, sweat, and tears into it. But there comes a time when you feel that pull in another direction.

I knew it was time for me to go, to move on to something else. I was at my parents' house—two hours from my home—with my little boy, who was still just an infant. Out of nowhere, I got another call. This time, it was someone I'd never met, offering me another flying job.

I remember thinking, "Really? Right now?" I was at dinner with my family. So, I told them I'd call back on Monday. And just like that, I had my next job.

I've never had to do the whole interview rigmarole, at least not in the traditional sense. In more than 30 years of flying, I've only sat through one job interview. People know who I am; my reputation speaks for itself. It's like there's this invisible network where names just get passed around. "Hey, so-and-so needs somebody," and somehow, my name comes up. I don't overthink it. If it fits, I go for it.

I've always lived by a simple motto: "If you can, you do; if you can't, you will." It's gotten me through some of the craziest times, moments where everything seemed to hang by a thread. It's a guiding principle that's helped me make decisions when others might have hesitated.

Whenever someone asks if I can do something, I say yes. You find a way; you figure it out. There's no room for doubt or second-guessing. You show up, and you get the job done. That's how it's always been for me.

Looking back, there were moments when I could have played it safe, stayed where things were comfortable. But that's just not who I am. Life keeps throwing me curveballs, and I keep swinging. Sometimes I miss, but more often than not, I connect.

There's a thrill in not knowing what's coming next, in being ready for whatever challenge presents itself. Despite all the unpredictability, I wouldn't have it any other way.

Even now, I'm ready for the next call, the next opportunity that might come out of the blue. It's the way my life has always been—a series of unexpected events, each leading to the next chapter. And somehow, through all the chaos, it always seems to work out.